Heal Yourself Naturally
BENTONITE CLAY

Nancy Stine

April, 2012
All Rights Reserved
Printed in the United States of America

TABLE OF CONTENTS

ACKNOWLEDGMENTS

My special thanks go to my daughter, Renee M Angus, who spent many hours helping me to edit and rebuild this book. She taught me to build my next book within the framework of an outline. Thank you, Renee. I think she shuddered, "Oh, no!" when I said I was thinking of my next book.

And I want to thank all my kids, Kris, Darrin, Wayne and Renee for being there for me at a time when I was ill and needed them most. As soon as my kids found out about the healing power of clay they insisted among themselves that I at least get a fighting chance to live and they saw to it that I got my daily therapy of clay when I couldn't prepare the clay myself.

And a thank you to their spouses who so generously supported them when they needed that support. God bless you all.

INTRODUCTION

If you had been given thirteen additional free years of life and, in the bargain, discovered a powerful new alternative tool to fixing old health problems like stomach problems, infections, and numerous other annoying ailments, wouldn't you want to tell the world about this amazing tool so they could be using it too? Bentonite clay is that amazing tool. Bentonite clay saved my life.

I was first introduced to the clay at Tecopa Hot Springs where my sister and I would visit on weekends. Many of the snowbirds who winter at the hot springs use the clay for their various ailments, as well as bathe in the healthy hot springs water. Since finding out about the clay my family and I started using it as well.

No claims have been made that Bentonite clay is the "Fountain of Youth" - that you will grow younger and live forever. All I know is that I use it. I'm alive today because of Bentonite clay.

In January of 1999 I was taken by ambulance to emergency with a double dissected aortal aneurysm and renal aneurysm. The aortal wall is layered like an onion. I had three spiral tears going down the length of my aortal wall; thus, three layers of my aortal wall were destroyed. Once my blood pressure (which was rapidly spiking and falling) became stabilized, the next concern was bypass surgery to repair the aorta. I chose to not accept the 6 to 8 units of blood that were to be on standby for the surgery due to my religious beliefs. The doctors from two hospitals threw up their hands in frustration. They refused to do the surgery without the safety net of blood transfusions. They **could not** do the surgery without blood transfusions.

A couple days later I was moved to a hospice care center – to die. I was totally out of my mind due to the toxicity building up from my body's sensitivity to the medications I was given.

Toxicity was going to take me out before the dissected aortal aneurysms would. It was at this time that my kids found out just how strong the healing powers of clay are. They would not accept my dying without a fight. They started me on a daily regime of clay water. After a couple days, I began to come out of the dense fog I was in. They took me home to die.

In April of 1999, just 3 months after my aneurysms emergency, I had an MRI and a conference at Cleveland Heart Clinic to talk about bloodless surgery. I was told, "You are not even a candidate for surgery. Your aneurysms are 3.3 to 3.4 cm. in diameter. We don't even consider surgery until they are 5 to 6 cm. in diameter, or growing rapidly. They didn't even mention my aortal wall. Obviously, the aortal wall had healed.

Today, as I write this in mid 2012, I am still alive and healthy – and I have had 13 blessed free years given to me. I flunked two hospices.

Bad times may SOON be coming! As the survivalist preppers are stashing up food, supplies, solar generators, etc to get them and their families through a natural disaster, loss of power grid, an economic breakdown or whatever may happen, so also must we be "prepping" to become self sufficient for our health care needs.

We will be on our own – left to our own resources as far as our health care is concerned. We may not have access to doctors or hospitals or prescription drugs. That's where a knowledge of alternative health care choices will come in handy. By putting into practice these alternative health care choices we can be reducing our dependence on doctors right now.

Bentonite clay may well be one of those alternative health care choices.

CHAPTER 1 - THE HEALING POWERS OF CLAY

Cultures throughout the ages have relied on the healing powers of clay. It's quite possible that early man was a clay eater. The Egyptians used clay for health care and to mummify their dead. The Essenes (writers of the Dead Sea Scrolls) used it as a primary healing therapy. The Greek doctor, Dioscorides recognized clay as having an "extraordinary strength" for healing. Avicena, the Arab "Prince of Doctors" and Galen, the physician, widely used clay for healing. Both praised it highly. Pliny the Elder, Roman naturalist and writer, wrote about clay extensively in his "Natural History". Sebastian Kneipp, a Bavarian priest who was one of the founders of naturopathic medicine, used the clay for healing. Emanuel Felke, a German naturopath in the 1800s, often referred to as the clay pastor endorsed treatments including applications of clay and clay baths. Kuhn, Just, and other European naturopaths in the 1800s' used clay for healing. India's Mahatma Ghandi used clay for constipation . . . and Jesus healed with clay.

Cultures all over the world use clay for medicinal purposes. Missionaries to every continent have found the eating of clay by aboriginal people. You may have read about or seen televised documentaries about the Hunzakuts in Eastern Pakistan, the Georgians in Western Russia, the Vilcabambas, and the Titicaca Indians, high in the Andes Mountains of Ecuador and Peru, who routinely lived to be 120 years to 140 years old, living full, productive and enjoyable lives. There is one thing they all have in common. The high altitude places where each lives have soil that contains large amounts of Montmorillonite clay deposits. The food that is locally grown in this soil has been enriched because of it.

American Indian tribes in the southwestern United States used the healing clay internally and externally for their ailments. The Paiute and Shoshone Indians bathed in the muddy hot springs near Death Valley. Various Indian tribes in the valley atop the Big Horn Mountains in Wyoming depended on the clay found there. They called it Ee-Wah-Kee (the mud that heals).

Today the clay is still used medicinally by some Native American tribes as a part of their home remedies.

Many people today, particularly in the southeast part of the United States regularly use clay for healing, especially during pregnancy. And studies of local folkways throughout the United States and the world find groups of people who regularly are clay eaters.

Bathing in clay waters from the hot springs near Tecopa, California, is seeing a comeback with seniors who come there to overcome their arthritis symptoms. These snowbirds see such improvement over their physical health that they are able to maintain full and active lives and attend two dances a week.

CHAPTER 2 - WHAT IS BENTONITE

Throughout this book, I'm going to use the term Bentonite, but unless I specifically state otherwise, what I say goes for Bentonite, Montmorillonite, Pascalite, Fuller's Earth or Ee-Wah-Kee. In the following treatise, my research found that scientists, doctors, researchers, etc. often used the terms interchangeably. This book will not be getting into the intricacies of individual chemistries nor does it need to for our purposes.

Bentonite was named for the clay found in the Fort Benton series of cretaceous rocks in Wyoming. Montmorillonite was named for the French town of Montmorillon, France where it was first found. Pascalite was named for the trapper who found the clay in the high valley in the Big Horn Mountains in Wyoming. Bentonite is found predominately in western United States, but also in many other parts of the globe. It is a product of Mother Nature. It is not man-made.

Often one writer, telling of stories and describing results, physical properties, etc. will call the clay Bentonite while another writer or expert will tell the same story with the same results and call the clay Montmorillonite or Pascalite. That's understandable. Bentonite, Montmorillonite, and Pascalite are *names* of clays of the Smectite group of clays and sometimes trade names.

Smectite clays or combinations of layers of Smectite clays and other clays have both the qualities of adsorption and absorption. Clays in this group are called living clay. In a hydrous state, they act as a catalyst which awakens the latent energies in our body. They produce enzymes which cause actions to begin the body's healing process.

Minerals are the components of enzyme systems vital to the body's growth and healing processes. These mineral/enzyme systems protect the body against outside toxic inundation and to provide immunity against harmful microbes, viruses and other pathogens. Maureen Kennedy Salaman, "the first Lady of Nutrition" strongly advocated our need for minerals through her books, guest lectures, and television appearances.

Bentonite is made up of at least 65 major and trace minerals and often more than that. The amounts and types of minerals vary from one sample of clay to another because the clays are often a mixture of several of the seven groups of clay. A sample of Bentonite clay found in a Nevada mine was analyzed and found to have contained 74 trace elements.

Millions of years ago the soil on our earth's surface was saturated with many minerals - between 84 to 100 minerals in some places. It stands to reason that God must have put those minerals in the soil for a purpose. When man began to till the soil, especially in the last 100 years, wind, rain erosion, and continuous crops gradually caused the soils to lose minerals. Thus, the foods we get from these mineral-poor soils have little nutritional value.

Man began to add artificial fertilizers to their crops – combinations of nitrate, phosphate and potash. This resulted in crop yields that could be greatly increased. According to the COMPLETE BOOK OF MINERALS FOR HEALTH by Rodale Press, ". . . man-made fertilizers upset the delicate balance of minerals and organisms in humus rich soil by killing off the beneficial bacteria. Man-made fertilizers lack in the naturally occurring minerals, therefore, these minerals are less available to plants." Plant roots can become saturated with one nutrient and miss picking up other minerals that they need.

Thus, we need to look elsewhere for the minerals our bodies need. Bentonite (the clay that heals) is a 100% natural combination of colloidal silicate minerals. It is formed from weathered volcanic ash and ancient oceanic sediment which consists of seaweed, algae and other calciferous marine life. Volcanic actions are believed to have brought these minerals to the surface to again be deposited in veins where the clay is often found. Normally, metallic minerals are hard to digest or assimilate; however the metallic minerals in Bentonite have already been assimilated or digested by the plants and are known as ***water soluble, plant derived, colloidal minerals***. In this state they are no longer harmful. These minerals are readily assimilated by the body. They are now beneficial to the body.

These clays have the greatest healing power because their particles, being shaped like a card with wide surfaces being negative and the edges of the card being positive, each particle has many times more negative than positive pulling power. This pulling power is adsorptive in action. *To **adsorb** is to collect (a gas, liquid or dissolved substance) in condensed form on a surface. This adsorptive action is what aids in detoxification of the intestinal canal. Think of this adsorbent action as a ball with negative ions that magnetically pulls the positive ions of toxins tightly to its surface. But, Bentonite clay also has absorbent action, which is a much slower action. *To **absorb** is to suck up or drink in as a blotting paper absorbs ink. By absorbent action, this ball now soaks up those positive ions into itself by a "sucking in" action, thus holding the "bad" ions in suspension until the body rids itself of them. This is a physical action, not a chemical one.

The minute quality of the particles of Bentonite clays gives each particle a large surface area in proportion to the volume used thus enabling it to pick up many times its own weight in positively charged particles.

CHAPTER 3 - HOW DOES BENTONITE WORK?

Bentonite clay is being used, more and more as a "healing clay". People are drinking clay activated water for general well-being. Even more are drinking it for their flu, hay fever, stomach problems, diarrhea or constipation, sore throats and gums. Many are putting it on their burns, scrapes, infections and open sores. Their burns don't blister. Their pain is relieved. Their infections and sores are healing up. Their colonic problems, whether diarrhea or constipation, or irritable bowel syndrome are becoming normalized. Gastrointestinal problems are noted for not being noticed anymore. Heartburn and acid reflux seem to have disappeared. The eyes are brighter. The step is livelier. One day, one may notice that he hasn't sneezed even though its prime allergy season - but his usual allergies aren't there. He feels better.

Clay works on the entire body – wherever it is needed. It is not an overnight cure but the beginning of a chain reaction. For this reason, once you begin treatment, continue its use until the process is complete. When beginning clay treatments, often as the chain reaction begins, the treated area may initially look worse or feel worse. This is due to the stirring up of toxins. When the body detoxifies, there is often an apparent change for the worse. This is called a **healing crisis**. This often happens especially in chronic conditions because massive accumulation of toxic wastes end up in the tissues. You probably will feel worse before you feel better. You may experience *skin eruptions, headaches, bad breath, foul smelling bowel movements, nasal discharge, fever, pain in the joints.* You may seem to be passing gas a lot.

Continue use of the clay. Improvement will soon become evident as the toxins in your body are removed by the clay within 2 or 3 days or sometimes even overnight.

There is a reason for this healing crisis. Paavo Airola, in his book, HOW TO GET WELL - Dr. Airola's HANDBOOK OF

NATURAL HEALING, tells us that any detoxification program, whether it is juice fasting, a cleansing diet, or the clay in this instance, in its detoxification process, "will dissolve huge amounts of accumulated toxins and debris and throw them into the bloodstream for elimination. The eliminative organs -- kidneys, liver, lungs, and skin -- will be overloaded with work." This is not the time to quit the program. This healing crisis is temporary. Dr. Airola tells us, "Eventually, the patient will experience a definite improvement as the body will cleanse itself of the accumulated poisons and become strong enough to initiate an effective healing activity."

Bentonite clay is not a drug. It doesn't work like a drug. Per Ran Knishinski in THE CLAY CURE, "Clay binds with and removes body toxins in the stomach, small intestine, and colon. It also stimulates the normal mechanism of the intestinal tract. In this way, it activates the immune system to defend itself against illness caused by too long an exposure to harmful poisons that accumulate in the bowel." This action of **synergism** in clay's minerals is what is the healing power of clay. *The SECOND COLLEGE EDITION OF THE AMERICAN HERITAGE DICTIONARY defines **synergism** as being "the action of two or more substances to achieve an effect, of which each alone is incapable."

Dr. Donsbach tells us, in WHAT YOU ALWAYS WANTED TO KNOW ABOUT ACNE REVISED that, "One of the most important factors in any disease condition is the detoxification of the body. It follows that such a detoxification can be an excellent means of preventing disease and promoting good health."

Every day we are being bombarded by poisons in our environment thus causing a build-up of toxins in our bodies. Toxins such as corn syrup, white sugar and sugar substitutes, hormones in our meat, chemicals and dyes in our beauty products, tobacco (whether we are smokers or from second hand smoke), alcohol, caffeine, prescription drugs, over-the counter drugs, recreational drugs, pesticides, automobile exhaust pollution, industrial pollution, municipal water, cleaning products, food additives, and radiation from our microwaves, TVs and computers. No wonder we are a disease-prone nation. No wonder we need the detoxifying powers of clay to rid our bodies of all these poisons.

Bentonite clay's action in detoxifying the body, thus aiding the body to heal itself is due to several characteristics:

- It has a large mineral count.

- It has a negative electrical attraction for positively charged particles. (In the human body, many of the toxic poisons are positively charged.)

- Much of clay's healing action is due to its property of synergism. It acts as a catalyst and enhances the production of enzymes that further promote healing action.

CHAPTER 4 - VERY IMPORTANT INFORMATION

Reap the positive benefits of natural healing clay without the worry of harmful side effects. One of the great advantages of clay is that it has never been known to adversely affect existing conditions such as high blood pressure, diabetes or allergies – or any other ailment. Independent studies have indicated no ill effects when intake does not exceed 25% of the total diet.

Clay is living, a product of mother earth. It is energized by the sun and needs to breathe. Do not use a tightly closed lid on the clay powder or refrigerate.

When you get your clay, if it is in a plastic bag, take it out of the bag and place it in a bowl or jar (glass, ceramic, earthenware, or porcelain, but not metal). To allow the clay to breathe, cover loosely with a napkin or cheesecloth, etc.

Clay is deactivated by metal because of its negative charge. Always use a plastic spoon or a wooden tongue depressor when measuring out and stirring the clay. **Do not use a metal spoon.**

BE SURE TO DRINK LOTS OF WATER!!! This will help the kidneys to get rid of this accumulation of toxins.

*IF YOU TAKE MEDICATIONS – Do not take the medications and clay at the same time. Allow a 2 hour time span between the taking of clay and your medications.

Having a multitude of uses, clay can successfully be used both internally as well as externally. It can be applied as a powder, thin paste or a thick poultice. It can be mixed with water alone or water and a little lemon juice and drank. Clay is sometimes eaten in the form of clay balls.

FOR EXTERNAL USE:

To make clay paste, use 1 part clay powder to 2 parts water. A glass jar (with a plastic lid) is a good container. Shake it up and let it set for at least 10 minutes. In order to keep the clay paste from drying out you will need to use a plastic lid and/or cover with plastic wrap.

For burns, scrapes, insect bites, etc, using fingers or a rubber spatula spread a thick layer of clay paste on the affected area. Keeping the clay poultice moist will reduce scabbing over of the wound and residual scarring. One way to do this is by wrapping the affected area in plastic wrap. You may then wrap the area with an ace bandage loosely to hold the plastic wrap in place. This keeps the clay from drying out and flaking off. In a few hours rinse this off with water and reapply clay dressing if necessary. Do this 2 or 3 times a day.

For tooth and gum infection make a thicker paste and form it into a ball and place it between your cheek and gum.

For diaper rash put clay powder in an empty talc can and sprinkle on area. Rinse at each diaper change and reapply.

*After clay has been used, throw it away. It is full of toxins and devitalized.

FOR INTERNAL USE:
Measure one or two teaspoons clay in a water glass. Or you can make it up in a 2 quart pitcher and keep it in the refrigerator to drink throughout the day. Stir (no metal spoons) and allow it to settle for at least 10 minutes. Drink the water off the top clear or stir it again and drink it cloudy. The clay water should have a bland dusty taste.

Drink lots of water while you are using the clay in order to help your body rid itself of the toxins that are being stirred up by the clay. *Note the repetition here. :-)

Clay may be used internally to help with a crisis like food poisoning or, as an ongoing therapy to stabilize your body's systems. With prolonged use you may see benefits and relief from chronic conditions that medical doctors find difficult to treat. Since the body's use of the clay's minerals works synergistically – by using the clay daily it can help chronic conditions and you may notice a gradual reduction of symptoms.

People who have tried the clay have often found that they notice a relief from their symptoms after they use the clay. Some uses for the clay include the following:

Acne, itching, hives
Allergies and hay fever
Anemia
Arthritis and rheumatism
Athlete's foot/jock itch
Bad breath
Boils
Burns
Chronic fatigue syndrome
Circulatory problems
Cradle cap
Diaper rash
Diverticulitis
Eczema
Food poisoning
Gum disease: gingivitis and pyorrhea
Heavy metals poisoning
Hemorrhoids
Hepatitis and cirrhosis
Insect bites and stings
Intestinal parasites
Irritable bowel syndrome
Liver problems
Menstrual cramps
Nursing mother's sore nipples
Prostate problems

Stomach ulcers
Strep throat
Sunburn
Yeast infection

And probably many more health concerns.

The pendulum is swinging back to using Nature's products for healing. Why did it take so long for us to learn about the "old ways"? Often, trying to reinvent the wheel, we are blinded to the effectiveness of the age old cures of our ancestors.

In my Bibliography I include links to many of the actual articles and books from which I obtained my information for this book. Don't miss this valuable source for more information. **I also include sources for purchasing the clay.**

CHAPTER 5 – TESTIMONIALS

I have another incident where clay has come to my rescue in a big way. - About 10 months ago I severely injured my right leg by getting it caught between the wheel and buggy body. The horse was raring and my ankle kept getting twisted more. It was amazing that the ankle wasn't broken; however it was greatly bruised. Since I am diabetic my doctor was very concerned about the injury and has been keeping close watch over the following months. The leg and ankle has been quite discolored and looked different from the other leg and had been hard and cold to the touch.

Three weeks ago the front of the leg started oozing a clear liquid. This scared me because I suspected it might be gangrene or something serious like that. Of course I noticed this oozing on a Friday evening so I couldn't schedule a doctor's appointment until the following Monday. I spread a thick layer of the clay over my leg and covered it with plastic wrap. Then I wrapped the leg with an ace bandage loosely. The next day the leg was still oozing fluid so I repeated the treatment. After 2 more days and overnights of treating the leg with clay the oozing of fluid had stopped – and the color of the leg has lightened to a normal flesh color and the skin feels normal to the touch."

Another example of the power of clay to relieve the itching of multiple mosquito bites follows. - My sister and I were traveling from Nevada cross country in a motor home. In Illinois we enjoyed Fourth of July fireworks on a park hillside on a hot, humid evening. The mosquitoes were thick – and biting. We were covered with itching mosquito bites. After retiring to the motor home we applied a paste of clay to the insect bites. All itching and discomfort stopped."

Bentonite clay is in my medicine chest. I use it for everything. I use it for burns. They don't blister. I use it for cuts, sore throats, nausea, vomiting, flu, colds, bee stings, insect bites, and sunburn. Whatever I use the clay for, it works."

Renee A - "Two years ago I had five back yard chickens. Someone gave me a chicken who had a crossed beak and a terrible infestation of scaly leg mites. These mites get under the scales of their legs and feet causing the scales to be raised, swollen and tender. Emmy immediately descended to last on the pecking order for food as she raised each foot and closed it in pain from walking or standing.

I separated her from the other hens and used traditional methods to kill mites, fleas and ticks quickly. Next, I applied a thick paste of hydrated clay to her feet and legs about every 2 to 3 days. I hand fed her the leftover clay paste which she seemed to enjoy. Then I dusted the chicken coop and nests with Diatomaceous Earth (DTE) to prevent any further infestations.

I continued the treatments weekly to Emmy's feet and legs for the rest of summer, but I noticed a big improvement in Emmy after the first week. She was laying eggs regularly. It took a while , but she eventually worked her way up the pecking order, passing a small pullet who was very shy and skittish. Emmy was happy and healthy. She became my granddaughter's favorite chicken because she liked to be held and the crossed beak made her look cute.

*note: Diatomaceous Earth (DTE) is not a clay, but a natural occurring fossil that, when ground into fine dust kills many insects without chemicals by getting under their shells. If the chickens accidently ate some, the results would be that it also kills parasites inside their digestive tracts. You must use *food grade* DTE, not pool grade. DTE can also be used to dust your dogs and cats for fleas and it kills bedbugs."

Kris M – "I crushed my finger in the door of my van. I should have gone to emergency – it was that severe. I suffered excruciating pain and throbbing for the next two days, applying triple antibiotic ointment and a dressing – with no relief. The finger looked worse than the day I crushed it. It was extremely swollen and very painful. On the evening of the third day a friend suggested I apply a thick paste of the clay to the finger. I did this and went to bed. The next morning upon rising I noticed there was something considerably different about my finger. I unwrapped it and to my amazement the finger looked like it had been healing for 3 weeks. The swelling (although still there) was considerably less. After using the clay on my finger for about a week, the finger returned to near normal size and all the cuts were healed and most of the bruising had gone, although I did still lose my fingernail."

Kris M - "On Easter Sunday, while preparing Easter dinner, my husband removed a roasting pan from the hot oven. Not realizing the pan was freshly out of the oven, I grabbed it and started across the room. You could hear my hands sizzling. Racked with pain I returned the pan to the stovetop. Dropping it I rushed to the sink and turned on the cold water to relieve the pain. Everywhere my hands and fingers had touched the pan - were burned badly. After applying a thick layer of clay to my hands the pain lessened a lot after 5 or 10 minutes. Wearing a pair of white gloves I ate dinner and by early evening the pain was nearly gone. I applied more clay before going to bed and again the next day. By the second day all signs of the burn were gone and there were no blisters."

Kris M – "I had a fungal infection on the right side of my lower back for several years. I tried over-the-counter medications, and finally went to the doctor who gave me a prescription which seemed to work. However as soon as the medication was gone the fungal infection would come right back. I went through several refills of the prescription with the same results. Then I decided to give the clay a try. After 2 days the infection was gone and to this day has not returned."

Kris M - "One morning I awoke to a bad toothache. I knew what it was because I have had it before. An abscess had built up from a very painful tooth and gum condition. I had bought some clay a few days earlier so I made a clay ball and placed it in my mouth back by the infected tooth. By that evening the tooth was feeling much better. I applied some more clay and went to bed. By the next morning the pain and swelling were gone and my tooth and gum were almost back to normal. After 2 more days of treatment all symptoms were completely gone and after several months had not returned. Just a few pennies worth of clay saved me several hundred dollars worth of dental treatment. However, eventually I had to have the tooth pulled."

Jerry M – I have suffered from heartburn and acid reflux every day no matter what I ate. At night I would awaken choking and gagging from acid reflux. Then one day I decided to try the clay. To my amazement I have had no more problems with acid reflux or heartburn since beginning the clay treatment. I have also noticed that my allergies have been greatly reduced. No more watery eyes, and very little sneezing. I used to have attacks of sneezing almost every day, sometimes 6, 8, or 10 in a row. But now a sneeze is a rare occurrence and my runny nose has lessened to almost nothing."

Duke S - "During deer season I received a bug bite on my ankle. It kept getting bigger so I put some iodine on it and, to my horror, the size nearly doubled to about the size of a silver dollar. This continued for several months with no relief. I also had some skin lesions on each temple, and figuring they were from advancing years, I thought that nothing could be done about them. Then my wife heard about the clay from a friend and I decided to give it a try. Within 3 days the bite had cleared up and has not returned – and within 3 weeks the lesions on my temple have completely disappeared also."

Duke's wife, Dee - "After seeing the results that Duke had, I decided to give the clay a try. I had not had regular bowel movements for over 40 years, bouncing back and forth between diarrhea and constipation. Within a couple days of drinking the clay water I was regular again and I have been regular ever since."

Linda, a nurse - "My husband, Dave had a large scratch running the length of his left forearm which was a couple days old. It had a bad staph infection and was all swollen and red. Medications prescribed by the doctor were not helping. I convinced my skeptical husband to try clay. He applied some, let it dry, and then washed it off. He applied more before going to bed that evening. Upon rising he went to the bathroom and washed off the clay. To his amazement the infection was completely gone. He was so excited that he woke me to show me the results. After one more day of treatment the scratch was gone."

Linda - " I decided to try some of the clay just for general well being. After a few days of using the clay I feel more energetic and less tired."

Wanda had toe surgery. The doctor told her the toe would take a couple months to heal. Her daughter put some clay on the toe and wrapped it which soothed and lessened the pain. After a couple of days her toe was feeling much better. Within a week her toe had healed enough that she could wear shoes comfortably.

Maury G from Tecopa Hot Springs, CA - "A man arrived at the hot springs with gangrene in one leg. He was unable to walk. His infected leg was discolored and there was a draining, open sore near his ankle. He was scheduled for surgery to have the leg removed. He began soaking the leg in water from the hot springs and Bentonite every day for several hours. The drainage from the open sore stopped within two days. He chose to miss the appointment to have surgery, choosing instead to continue his self-initiated treatment. Within six weeks his leg was normal and he went back to work as usual."

Maury G - "A man came to the hot springs with a severe case of rosacea. His nose was bulbous, inflamed red, and enlarged. Once, very sociable, this man became a recluse. He began applying a paste made from the clay and the hot springs water. After a week the rosacea was no longer there. His red nose returned to a normal color."

A lady in Utah had a severe case of psoriasis. She mixed the clay with water to make a thick paste and applied it to the psoriasis. After it dried she ran warm water over it washing it off. She then applied peroxide to the area, washed this off and dried it. Nights she would apply the clay paste and wrap her legs in plastic wrap. Four months later the lesions were gone. There was no scarring.

Jackie T, from Las Vegas - "Molly, my black lab retriever, had a severe rash on her belly and the underside of her body. I regularly dusted her with clay powder. Molly seemed to know the clay was going to help her and lifted her legs for me to apply the clay. After a few dustings the rash went away. Molly now gets clay in her drinking water once a day for general well-being."

Jackie T - "Our sister, Lee's jaw started swelling fast. Her doctor diagnosed it as a parotid gland tumor. A biopsy was scheduled to discover whether it was malignant or not but meanwhile Lee began drinking the clay water cloudy. Almost muddy. By biopsy date the swelling had gone down and Lee's face was normal again."

These are just a few of the stories that we have been told by people who have tried Bentonite clay, the clay that heals. There are many more such amazing stories out there. Bentonite is not a cure all, or a replacement for sound medical treatment. But for symptoms of chronic gastrointestinal ailments, minor aches and pains, tooth and gum problems, infections and more, clay treatment has proven to be very effective. Again, this is informational material only. The remedies, approaches, and techniques described are meant to educate and supplement, and are not a substitute for professional medical care or treatment.

APPENDIX - SCIENTIFIC PROOF THAT BENTONITE WORKS

Hydrated Bentonite, used by the Indians and many other cultures for thousands of years has been proven scientifically sound. A team of medical doctors performed clinical work using hydrated Bentonite in the treatment of a group of 35 patients who had diarrhea. The diarrhea was caused by virus infections, food allergy, spastic colitis, and food poisoning. Liquid Bentonite provided substantial relief in 97% of the cases. MEDICAL ANNALS of the DISTRICT OF COLUMBIA, Vol. 20. No. 6, June, 1961 - "The Value of Bentonite for Diarrhea".

As noted in the article, the doctors conclude that "By virtue of its physical action, Bentonite serves as an adsorbent aid in detoxification of the intestinal canal."

To back up the findings of the clinical experiments using Bentonite to detoxify the intestinal tract, in 1961, Dr. Howard E. Lind, president of Lind Laboratories in Brookline, Massachusetts, conducted laboratory experiments with hydrated Bentonite, "illustrating the mechanics of how it acts as an aid in detoxification via the alimentary tract".

Experiment I shows the extreme changes in bacteria population of a culture of SERRATIA MARCESCENS treated with a Bentonite preparation. These trials show a "minimum reduction of 85% and a maximum reduction of 99% of the bacteria in 90 minutes".

Experiment II was conducted with ESCHERICHIA COLI (a gram-negative organism) and STAPHYLOCOCCUS AUREUS (a gram-positive organism) treated with a Bentonite preparation. Bottom line - "the two trials show that the E.COLI was reduced 100% and 91% respectively after 60 to 90 minutes. The bacteria counts of STAPHYLOCOCCUS AUREUS, however, showed that S. AUREUS were reduced 21%, 39%, and 40% respectively, or an average of 33%".

Experiment III was a two-part experiment, conducted with PROTEUS MIRABILIS and a preparation of Bentonite, and, second, Bentonite "selective sorptive value in a mixture of PROTEUS MIRABILIS, (gram-negative), ESCHERICHIA COLI (gram-negative), and STAPHYLOCOCCUS AUREUS (gram-positive).

"In the trials with PROTEUS MIRABILIS and a Bentonite preparation, the bacterial count was reduced 100% after 90 to 120 minutes. In the second part of the experiment, "the Bentonite preparation removed from 95-100% of PROTEUS MIRABILIS, 83-100% of E. COLI, and 100% of S. AUREUS. ". . . there appeared to be selective sorption when the quantity of organism concentration was much less than the high concentration used in previous tests".

CONCLUSION

In this book I have explained what Bentonite clay is, how it works and why it works. I have shown that testing has been done and the experiments that were conducted prove that the clay works scientifically. I have shown how people throughout the ages and from all over the world have used the clay. And I have included several stories from people who use the clay today and the results they have obtained.

Along with having Bentonite clay as a powerful alternative to medicine and emergencies when/if the SHTF there are a few other common sense actions you can take to maintain your wellness during these precarious times.

- Learn deep breathing exercises to oxygenate your cells.
- Often when we feel symptoms such as arthritis or headache or high blood pressure it is your body's cries for water. Don't treat thirst with medications. Drink more water.
- Get enough sleep so that you can wake up in the morning naturally without an alarm clock and feel refreshed and ready for a new day.
- Keep moving, whether it is by exercising or walking or working.
- Keep a sunny outlook on life. The actions of prepping for the unknown alleviate fear of the unknown and promote a feeling of control over your life.
- Keep a positive spiritual point of view.
- These actions are free – simple, but are not necessarily easy.
- Here's to your good health!

BIBLIOGRAPHY

Abehsera, Michael. THE HEALING CLAY 1977, 1979

Dextreit, Raymond. EARTH CURES: A Handbook of Natural Medicine for Today 1997

Dr. Donsbach. WHAT YOU ALWAYS WANTED TO KNOW ABOUT ACNE REVISED 1980

Eaton, Jason R. BENTONITE: AN EDUCATIONAL COMPILATION. Public research project. July 9, 1995

Knishinsky, Ran. THE CLAY CURE: Natural Healing from the Earth. Healing Arts Press. Rochester, VT. 1998

Medical Annals of the District of Columbia, Vol.20.No. 6, June, 1961. THE VALUE OF BENTONITE FOR DIARRHEA

Rodale Press THE COMPLETE BOOK OF MINERALS FOR HEALTH

Paavo Airola HOW TO GET WELL - Dr. Airola's HANDBOOK OF NATURAL HEALING

Sources for the purchase of clay:

Your local health food store
Redmond Clay www.redmondclay.com   Redmond Clay has a lot of helpful videos.

The Living Clay Company www.livingclayco.com   Living Clay Company has a useful database.

My favorite source of vitamins www.puritan.com also has the clay.

There are probably other sources for the clay. Do a Google search.

ABOUT THE AUTHOR

 Nancy Stine, the author of "Survival Medicine" brings to the table: certification as a Nutritional Consultant, and many classes and seminars on health-related subjects such as Biokinesiology, Position Release, Touch For Health, Therapeutic Massage, Anatomy & Physiology, Microbiology, Pharmacology, Nursing Arts, Vitamins/Minerals/Herbs/Bach Flowers/Homeopathy/Cell Salts, and various other holistic related. Her series, "Heal Yourself Naturally " came about as research of the clay as the result of a personal experience with the clay's healing powers. She wanted to learn what makes the clay's powers of healing.

Stine is 80 years young, and has a background in nursing care and health and wellness. For several years she was a nutritional consultant/reflexologist/massage therapist using the techniques of holistic health. Alternative health care and taking charge of her own health care have been long time interests.

Nancy Stine, who has raised four children, enjoys the clean air and open spaces of the countryside, residing just outside Flint, MI. She is an avid reader and internet research is a hobby. She also occasionally researches family genealogies, scrapbooks, and enjoys camping with her family and spending time with her grandchildren and great grandchildren.

She recently authored a children's book series - Benji and Poppy Children's Books - which emphasizes the loving and enjoyable relationships between grandparents and their grandchildren.

Made in the USA
Middletown, DE
27 October 2017